WHAT CHRISTIANS BELIEVE

J. WESLEY EBY, EDITOR

f

THE FOUNDRY
PUBLISHING®

CONTENTS

Introduction   5

Lesson No.   Lesson Title

1   God Is the One True God   6
2   God Is the Creator   8
3   God Is a Great God   10
4   God Is Holy and Loving   12
5   God Is Triune   14
6   God Gave Us the Holy Bible   16
7   The Bible Helps Us Live for God   18
8   People Are Sinful   20
9   Sin Is Disobeying God   22
10 God Is Our Judge   24
11 Jesus Christ Is the Perfect Sacrifice   26
12 God Forgives Our Sins   28
13 Jesus Christ Is God   30
14 Jesus Died, Yet He Lives   32
15 Jesus Is Coming Again   34
16 How to Become a Christian   36

Teaching Resources   38
Appendix A: Answers to Questions and Additional Scriptures   39
Appendix B: Word List   47
Appendix C: Teaching Helps   51

INTRODUCTION

This book is for people who are learning English. The sentences are short. The words are small. This should help you understand the lessons.

The writers want you to know about God. They want you to know about the Bible. And they want you to understand what you are learning. This is why the book was written.

You will learn what Christians believe in this book. You will learn about God. You will learn about Jesus Christ. You will learn about the Bible. You will learn about sin. And you will learn how to become a Christian.

Your pastor or teacher will help you learn. They want you to know about God. They want you to understand the Bible. So, ask them for help. Ask them about the things that you do not understand.

God loves you very much. He wants to be your God. He wants you to learn about Him. You can pray to God. You can ask Him to help you. He will help you understand. He will help you learn.

1 GOD IS THE ONE TRUE GOD

Important Bible Verse: "I am the **Lord**. There is no other God; I am the only God. . . ." (Isaiah 45:5)

God is the only God. He said: "I am the **Lord**. There is no other God; I am the only God. . . ." (Isaiah 45:5)

God is **powerful**. God has more power than any person. He is more **powerful** than any human king. God can do everything that He decides to do. No person can take away the power of God.

God keeps His promises. God does only what is right. He never does wrong. He does not do bad things. God is always good.

God made the earth. He made all people. God could make all people **worship** Him. But He does not do that. God lets us choose to **worship** Him.

God wants us to **worship** Him. God does not want us to **worship** other **gods**. Other **gods** are made by people. These **gods** are false **gods**. God said, "You must not have any other **gods** except Me." (Exodus 20:3)

God made us, and He knows us. He knows when we are happy. He knows when we are sad. God knows everything about us.

God loves us. He wants to help us. We talk to God when we pray. God listens to our prayers. He answers our prayers.

God does not sleep. God does not leave us. He is always near.

We learn other names of God in the **Bible**. The **Bible** calls Him Father. The **Bible** calls Him the **Lord**. The **Bible** calls Him King.

God is the great God. He is the only God. He is the one true God.

QUESTIONS: *Fill in the blanks.*

1. God is the only _____.
2. God says in Exodus 20:3, "You must not have

   _____ _____

   _____ except Me."
3. We can pray to _____.
4. God lets us _____ to **worship** Him.
5. God is called _____, the _____, and

   _____.

Give the answers.

6. Who has more power than any person? _____
7. Who listens to our prayers? _____
8. Who answers our prayers? _____
9. What did God make? He made the _____ and

   all _____.
10. What kind of God is God? He is the one _____

    God.

WORD LIST

1. **Bible** *(proper noun):* the book God gave us to learn about Him.
2. **gods** *(noun):* false gods; not the one true God.
3. **Lord** *(proper noun):* another name for God.
4. **powerful** *(adjective):* full of power; very strong.
5. **worship** *(verb):* to honor God; to praise and serve God.

2   GOD IS THE CREATOR

Important Bible Verse: "[He is] the God who made the whole world and everything in it. . . ." (Acts 17:24)

God made all things. The Bible says, "[He is] the God who made the whole world and everything in it. . . ." (Acts 17:24) The Bible tells the story of **creation**. You can read this story in Genesis chapters 1 and 2.

God is the **Creator. Creator** means that God makes something from nothing.

Our world did not just happen. The Bible says, ". . . God is the **builder** of everything." (Hebrews 3:4, NIV) God is the **builder** or **Creator** of all things.

God **created** day and night. God made the sky and the earth. He made the land and water. He made all plants and animals. He **created** people.

God made the first man. He made man from the soil of the earth. God breathed life into the body of the man. God **caused** the man to live.

Everything God **created** is good, The Bible says, "God looked at everything He had made, and it was very good. . . ." (Genesis 1:31)

God is **greater** than His **creation**. He **created** all people. He **created** the world for us. We are very important to God. God loves all His **creation**.

QUESTIONS: *Fill in the blanks.*

1. "[He is] the God who made the whole_____ and everything in it . . . ." (Acts 17:24)
2. God is the _____.
3. God is the **builder** of _____.
4. God breathed _____ into the body of man.
5. We are very _____ to God.
6. God loves all His _____.

Give the answers.

7. Who made all things? _____
8. What tells the story of **creation**? The _____
9. What did God make? _____
10. What did God use to make the first man? He used the _____ of the _____.

WORD LIST

1. **builder** *(noun):* a person who builds or makes something.
2. **caused** *(verb):* made to happen.
3. **created** *(verb):* made something from nothing.
4. **creation** *(noun):* everything God has made.
5. **Creator** *(proper noun):* a name for God, who made all things.
6. **greater** *(adjective):* more great; with more power.

3 GOD IS A GREAT GOD

Important Bible Verse: "The LORD your God is God of all gods and Lord of all lords. He is the great God. . . ." (Deuteronomy 10:17)

God has always lived. He lived before He made anything. The Bible says, ". . . before You created the earth and the world, You are God. You have always been, and you will always be." (Psalm 90:2) God has always been alive. He will never die.

God is a Spirit. People have bodies. But God does not have a body.

Everything on earth has a beginning and an end. People are born and people die. All plants and animals have a beginning and an end.

God said, "I am the **Alpha** and the **Omega,** the First and the Last, the Beginning and the End." (Revelation 22:13) This means that God is **eternal.** God is not like people, plants, and animals. He is the **Alpha** and the **Omega.** God did not have a beginning. And God will not have an end.

God is **everywhere.** God is **everywhere** at the same time. He is a Spirit. He is with us all the time. We can always pray to Him.

God is powerful. He has the power to create. He created the earth and the world. He has the power to give life. He has the power to heal. God is more powerful than any spirit or person.

God knows all things. He knows everything we do. He knows everything we think. We cannot hide anything from God. The Bible says, "Nothing in all the world can be **hidden** from God. . . . " (Hebrews 4:13)

God is **eternal.** He is **everywhere.** He is powerful. He knows all things. God is a great God. The Bible says, "The LORD your God is God of all gods and Lord of all lords. He is the great God. . . ." (Deuteronomy 10:17)

QUESTIONS: *Fill in the blanks.*

1. God has always _____.
2. God did not have a _____.
   And God will not have an _____.
3. God is _____ at the same time.
4. God is more _____ than any spirit or person.
5. "Nothing in all the _____ can be **hidden**
   from God. . . ." (Hebrews 4:13)

Give the answers.

6. What word means that God has no beginning and no end?
   _____
7. Where is God? _____
8. Who has the power to give life? _____
9. Who knows all things? _____
10. Why is God a great God? God is _____.
    He is _____. He is _____.
    He knows _____ _____.

WORD LIST

1. **Alpha** *(noun):* the first letter in the Greek alphabet. Alpha means the beginning.
2. **eternal** *(adjective):* has no beginning or end; has always lived and will always live.
3. **everywhere** *(adverb):* all places.
4. **hidden** *(adjective):* not seen with the eyes; not in sight.
5. **Omega** *(noun):* the last letter in the Greek alphabet. **Omega** means the end.

4 GOD IS HOLY AND LOVING

Important Bible Verse: "... I am the LORD your God. You must be holy because I am holy." (Leviticus 19:2)

God is a holy God. This means that God is not **evil**. He does no **evil** thing.

Holy also means **perfect**. Only God is holy and **perfect**. God said, "... I am the LORD your God. You must be holy because I am holy." (Leviticus 19:2)

People are not holy. People are **evil**. But God wants us to become holy. God said, "... I am the LORD your God. You must be holy because I am holy." (Leviticus 19:2) God will help us to become holy.

God is a **loving** God. The Bible says, "... God is love. . . . " (1 John 4:16) God loves us very much.

Many people worship false gods. But these gods do not have love. It is not easy to make these false gods happy. Only the one true God is a God of love.

God is a God of peace. The Bible says, "I [Jesus] leave you peace. My peace I give you. . . ." (John 14:27) The peace of God is deep inside us. His peace will make us **content**. Only God can give this peace to us.

The peace of God is a gift to us. We do not have to work for it. God gives us peace to help us live. We will be **content**. God will not become angry. He will not take our peace away.

God is holy and **perfect**. God is a **loving** God. And God gives peace.

QUESTIONS: *Fill in the blanks.*

1. God is a _____ God.
2. People are not holy. They are _____.
3. "... God is _____. ..." (1 John 4:16)
4. God loves us _____ _____.
5. The _____ of God is a gift to us.

Give the answers.

6. Who is holy? _____
7. What will God help us to become? _____
8. Who is the only God of love? the one _____
9. What will the peace of God make us?_____
10. What does God give us to help us live? _____

WORD LIST

1. **content** *(adjective):* happy; full of joy.
2. **evil** *(adjective):* very bad; not good.
3. **loving** *(adjective):* full of love.
4. **perfect** *(adjective):* without **evil**; does nothing wrong; does not make mistakes.

5 GOD IS TRIUNE

Important Bible Verse: ". . . in the name of the Father and the Son and the Holy Spirit." (Matthew 28:19)

God is the one true God. He created all things. God is great, and He is holy. We have learned many things about God.

Now, we will learn that God is **triune**. This means that He is **three in one**. This is not easy to understand. But God will help us understand it.

Many things can be **three in one**. A man can be **three in one**. He can be a father. He can be a son. He can be a brother also.

This is how God is **three in one**:

1. God shows us that He is our Father. He made us. He is our Creator. He loves and cares for us. The Bible says, ". . . You are my Father, my God . . ." (Psalm 89:26)

2. God shows us His love through His Son, Jesus Christ. Jesus is the Son of God. God sent Jesus Christ to earth because He loves us. Jesus came to show us the Father. Jesus said, "The Father and I are one." (John 10:30) ". . . Whoever has seen Me has seen the Father. . . ." (John 14:9)

3. God shows us that He is present with us. We call Him the Holy Spirit. He helps and **encourages** people. He helps us to know God. The Bible says, "But God has shown us these things through the [Holy] Spirit. The Spirit searches out all things. . . ." (1 Corinthians 2:10)

Jesus Christ talked about the **three in one**. He said, ". . . in the name of the Father and the Son and the Holy Spirit." (Matthew 28:19)

God is **triune**. He is the Father. He is the Son. And He is the Holy Spirit.

QUESTIONS: *Fill in the blanks.*

1. _____ is **triune.**
2. God sent Jesus Christ to earth because _____
   _____ _____.
3. _____ said, "The Father and I are one."
4. The Holy Spirit helps us to _____ God.
5. God is the _____, the _____,
   and the _____ _____.

Give the answers.

6. Who is great and holy? _____
7. What word means **three in one**? _____
8. Who made us? _____
9. Who came to show us God the
   Father?_____ _____
10. Whom did God send to **encourage** us? the
    _____ _____

WORD LIST

1. **encourage, encourages** *(verb):* make someone feel better;
   helps and guides.
2. **three in one** *(noun phrase):* three parts of one thing; the **triune**
   God.
3. **triune** *(adjective):* **three in one:** God is God in three persons:
   God the Father, God the Son, and God the Holy Spirit.

6   GOD GAVE US THE HOLY BIBLE

Important Bible Verse: "All **Scripture** is given by God . . ." (2
Timothy 3:16)

The Holy Bible is the **written** words of God. The Bible is called
Scripture. We call it the Word of God also. The Bible is **sacred**. It
is a holy book for **Christians**.

The Holy Bible is a large book. It has 66 smaller books. The
Bible has two parts. The Old Testament has 39 books. The New
Testament has 27 books.

The Old Testament tells about the creation. It tells us about
the laws of God. It also tells how God worked with people.

The New Testament tells about Jesus Christ, the Son of God.
It tells about the early church for **Christians**. It also tells us how
to live for God.

God tells us about **Himself** in the Bible. But God did not write
it with His own hand. God chose certain men to write His words.
These men wrote what God told them. The Bible says: "All Your
[God's] words are true. . . ." (Psalm 119:160, NIV)

God **inspired** the men who wrote the Bible. The Bible says,
". . . People led by the Holy Spirit spoke words from God." (2
Peter 1:21) "All **Scripture** is given by God . . ." (2 Timothy 3:16)
This makes the Bible the Word of God. This makes the Bible a
holy, **sacred** book.

People have **written** many good books. Some books tell the
truth about God. Today, we get help from these books. But they
are the words of people. They are not the **inspired** Word of God.

There is only one **inspired** Word of God. That book is the
Holy Bible. Every **Christian** should read the Bible. God speaks to
us today through the Bible. The Bible is complete. The Bible has
everything we need to know God.

QUESTIONS: *Fill in the blanks.*

1. The _____ _____ is the **written** words of God.

2. The Bible is called _____.

3. The _____ _____ tells about the creation and the laws of God.

4. The _____ _____ tells about Jesus Christ.

5. God _____ the men who wrote the Bible.

6. The Bible is complete. This means the Bible has _____ _____ _____ to know God.

Give the answers.

7. How many books are in the Bible? _____

8. In what does God tell us about **Himself**? the _____

9. What is given by God? (See 2 Timothy 3:16.) _____ _____

10. What is **inspired?** the _____

WORD LIST

1. **Christian, Christians** *(proper noun):* a person who believes Jesus Christ is the Son of God; people who follow and obey Jesus Christ.

2. **Himself** *(pronoun):* God talking as God.

3. **inspired** *(verb):* gave thoughts to; guided the mind.

4. **sacred** *(adjective):* holy; belonging to God.

5. **Scripture** *(proper noun):* **sacred written** words; special **written** words from God to all people; the Holy Bible for **Christians**.

6. **written** *(adjective):* in writing; put on paper so people can read.

7 THE BIBLE HELPS US LIVE FOR GOD

Important Bible Verse: "All Scripture is given by God and is **useful** for teaching, for showing people what is wrong in their lives. . . ." (2 Timothy 3:16)

The Holy Bible is a special book. It teaches us about God. It is the inspired Word of God. It is the Word of God to us. Now, we will learn more about the Bible.

There are many stories in the Bible. These stories are about people. Some people were bad. They did not obey God and His laws.

Other stories tell about good people. They obeyed God and His laws. They loved God. Life was sometimes **difficult** for them. These people prayed to God, and He helped them.

People do not always know how to live for God. The Bible teaches us how to live for God. The Bible says, "All Scripture is given by God and is **useful** for teaching, for showing people what is wrong in their lives. . . . (2 Timothy 3:16)

The Bible teaches that God loves everyone. The Bible says, "This is what real love is: . . . God's love for us." (1 John 4:10) God loved and helped the people of the Bible. Today, we can ask for His help too. God loves us very much. He will help us.

Sometimes, life is **difficult** for us. We are afraid or weak. The Bible can encourage us. It tells us that God is strong. He cares for us. The Bible says, ". . . He [God] cares for you." (1 Peter 5:7) God will **protect** and help us.

The Bible is from God. It is a **useful**, sacred book. We should read and study it. The Bible shows us the plan of God for our lives. It helps us live for Him every day.

QUESTIONS: *Fill in the blanks.*

1. The Bible _____ us about God.
2. The Bible teaches us how to _____ for God.
3. God _____ us very much.
4. God _____ for us. (1 Peter 5:7)
5. God will _____ and help us.
6. We should _____ and _____ the Bible.

Give the answers.

7. Who loves everyone? _____
8. What can we read to encourage us?
   the _____
9. Who can ask for the help of God?
   _____
10. What shows us the plan of God for our lives?
    the _____

WORD LIST

1. **difficult** *(adjective):* not easy; hard to do.
2. **protect** *(verb):* care for; keep safe.
3. **useful** *(adjective):* can be used; of help; helpful.

8 PEOPLE ARE SINFUL

Important Bible Verse: "I was brought into this world in **sin**. In **sin** my mother gave birth to me." (Psalm 51:5)

God is holy. God has no **sin.** He is not like false gods.

God made Adam and Eve without **sin.** They were the first people. They were the parents of all people. They were friends of God.

Satan is not the friend of God. **Satan** is not holy. He wants to hurt God. So **Satan tempted** Adam and Eve.

Satan told Adam and Eve not to obey God. Adam and Eve listened to **Satan.** They did not obey God. Adam and Eve **sinned.**

Sin changed the **nature** of Adam and Eve. They were not holy anymore. They did not want to live for God. They wanted to live their own way. Then, Adam and Eve were **sinful.** They had a **sinful nature.**

All people have come from Adam and Eve. So every person has a **sinful nature** also. The Bible says, "I was brought into this world in **sin.** In **sin** my mother gave birth to me." (Psalm 51:5) This means that we are born with **sin.** We are born with a **sinful nature.**

Sin separates us from God. The Bible says, "It is your evil that has **separated** you from your God. . . ." (Isaiah 59:2)

Our **sins** keep us away from God. The Bible says, "Our **sinful** selves want what is against the [Holy] Spirit, and the [Holy] Spirit wants what is against our **sinful** selves. The two are against each other. . . ." (Galatians 5:17)

Today, **Satan** still **tempts** us to **sin.** Our **sinful nature** makes it easy to **sin.** But our **sins separate** us from God.

QUESTIONS: *Fill in the blanks.*

1. God is holy. He has no _____.
2. Adam and Eve did not _____ God.
3. **Sin** changed the _____ of Adam and Eve.
4. Adam and Eve had a _____ **nature.**
5. **Sin** _____ us from God.

Give the answers.

6. Who were the first people? _____ and _____.
7. Who is **Satan?** He is not the _____
   _____ _____.
8. What did **Satan** do to Adam and Eve?
   He _____ them.
9. Who is born with **sin?** _____
10. What **separates** us from God? _____

WORD LIST

1. **nature** *(noun):* the real self; what a person is inside his being.
2. **Satan** *(proper noun):* the most powerful of evil spirits; Satan is against God and people.
3. **separates, separated** *(verb):* not together; apart; in two different places.
4. **sin; sins** *(noun):* evil; wrong acts.
   sin; sinned *(verb):* do wrong acts; did not obey God.
5. **sinful** *(adjective):* full of **sin.**
6. **sinful nature** *(noun phrase):* the part of people that makes them **sin.**
7. **tempts; tempted** *(verb):* tests; tried to get people to **sin** or do wrong.

9   SIN IS DISOBEYING GOD

Important Bible Verse: "All [people] have sinned . . ." (Romans 3:23)

We are all born with sin. We are sinful because Adam and Eve sinned. This means we have a sinful nature. This is one type of sin.

There is a second type of sin. Sin is choosing to **disobey** God. Sin is **disobeying** God. The Bible says, "All [people] have sinned . . . " (Romans 3:23) This means every person sins.

God gave many laws to us. Some laws tell us what to do. Some laws tell us what not to do. These laws help us not to sin. They help us to live good lives.

God gave ten special laws to us. They are called the Ten Commandments. God told us to worship only Himself. He told us to obey our parents. He told us not to steal and lie. You can read all the Ten Commandments in the Bible. (Read Exodus 20:1-17.)

Sin is **disobeying** the laws of God. The Bible says, "Everyone who sins **breaks the law** . . ." (1 John 3:4, NIV) Sin is **breaking the law** of God.

God is holy and pure. God does not sin. And God does not like sin. People are not holy when they sin. Sin separates people and God. People who sin are called **sinners.**

Sin is very bad. Sin causes people to do bad things. Sin causes people to **break the law** of God. The Bible says: ". . . I do not do what I want to do, and I do the things I hate . . . . It is sin living in me that does them." (Romans 7:15, 17)

God does not want people to sin. He wants to help **sinners.** He wants to be our friend.

QUESTIONS: *Fill in the blanks.*

1. We are all _____ with sin.
2. We are sinful because _____ and _____ sinned.
3. The laws of God help us live _____ _____.
4. Sin is _____ the laws of God.
5. God does not like _____.

Give the answers.

6. Who has sinned? _____
7. What do we call the ten special laws of God? the

   _____ _____
8. What do we call people who sin? _____

Answer with YES or NO. Circle the right answer.

9. Is sin choosing to **disobey** God?   YES or NO
10. Is stealing a sin?   YES or NO
11. Does God sin?   YES or NO
12. Does God want people to sin?   YES or NO

WORD LIST

1. **break the law, breaks the law, breaking the law** *(verb phrase):* **disobey** God; do not obey the laws of God.
2. **disobey, disobeying** *(verb):* do not obey; not obeying.
3. **sinners** *(noun):* people who sin; people who do not obey the laws of God.

10 GOD IS OUR JUDGE

Important Bible Verse: "Everyone must die once and be judged."
(Hebrews 9:27)

God wants to be our friend. But all sin separates us from God.

Our sinful nature is a **terrible** problem. It causes us to be against God. We do not want to listen to Him. We do not want to obey Him. We sin when we disobey God.

Sin brought death into the world. So all people die. God will judge all people after death. The Bible says, "Everyone must die once and be judged." (Hebrews 9:27)

We will go to the **judgment** after we die. God will judge us at the **judgment**. The Bible says, "We must all stand before Christ to be judged. . . . " (2 Corinthians 5:10) God will tell us where we will go then. Every person will go to **heaven** or **hell**.

God wants us to live with Him. He has made a place for us. This place is called **heaven**. The Bible says, "God made a promise to us, and we are waiting for a new **heaven** . . ." (2 Peter 3:13) But only holy people can live there.

God will send us away if we are not holy. We are sinners if we are not holy. Sinners belong to Satan. God will allow sinners to go to a **terrible** place called **hell**. The Bible says, ". . . Fear the one who has the power . . . to throw you into **hell**. Yes, this is the one you should fear." (Luke 12:5)

We cannot go to **heaven** because we are good. We cannot go to **heaven** because we do **good works**. We cannot go to **heaven** because we are nice. We must live holy lives. We must be friends with God. We must not be sinful.

But we are all sinners. We cannot stop sinning by **ourselves**. We need help. So God has a plan to help us. The Bible tells us about this plan.

QUESTIONS: *Fill in the blanks.*

1. All _____ separates us from God.
2. Sin brought _____ into the world.
3. All people die. God will _____ all people after death.
4. Every person will go to _____ or _____.
5. God has made a place for us. It is called _____.
6. We cannot go to **heaven** by doing _____ _____.
7. We must live _____ lives.
8. God has a _____ to help us.

Answer with a YES or NO. Circle the right answer.

9. Can we go to **heaven** by doing **good works?**   YES or NO
10. Do we live after we die?   YES or NO
11. Will sinners go to **heaven?**   YES or NO
12. Can we stop sinning by **ourselves?**   YES or NO

WORD LIST

1. **good works** *(noun phrase):* what we do to help other people; kind deeds.
2. **heaven** *(noun):* the place where God is; the home of God.
3. **hell** *(noun):* a place where people are punished forever for their sins; the home of sinners after death.
4. **judgment** *(noun):* when God will judge all people; when God says who goes to **heaven** or **hell.**
5. **ourselves** *(pronoun):* us; you and me.
6. **terrible** *(adjective):* very, very bad.

11 JESUS CHRIST IS THE PERFECT SACRIFICE

Important Bible Verse: "We are made holy through the **sacrifice** Christ made in His body once and for all time."' (Hebrews 10:10)

All people sin. They do not obey God. People cannot be friends with God because they sin.

People feel they should **please** God. So they give something to Him. This is called a **sacrifice**. But we cannot buy the love of God. We cannot buy His love with a **sacrifice**.

The best **sacrifice** is a blood **sacrifice**. It shows how people feel about their own sin. They know that they have disobeyed God. They want to **please** God. They want to be His friends.

People made blood **sacrifices** in **Bible times**. They used birds or animals to make blood **sacrifices**. They made **sacrifices** to **please** God.

But blood **sacrifices** are not enough. Anything a person does is not enough. The Bible says, "You did not save yourselves. . . . It was not the result of your own efforts, so you cannot brag about it." (Ephesians 2:8-9) Our good works are not enough. All people still sin.

Jesus Christ came to earth. He came to be the blood **sacrifice** for sin. He bled and died on a **cross**. He gave His life as the perfect **sacrifice**.

Jesus Christ died on a **cross** for everyone. The Bible says, "Christ died for all . . ." (2 Corinthians 5:15) This means that Jesus Christ died for all people. He died to **save** us from sin.

Jesus Christ is the plan of God for sin. Jesus **saves** us from sin and hell. He is our **Savior**.

We do not need to give blood **sacrifices** today. Jesus Christ was our **sacrifice**. The **sacrifice** of Jesus was enough. No other **sacrifice** is needed.

The Bible says, ". . . we are made holy through the **sacrifice** Christ made in His body once and for all time." (Hebrews 10:10) Jesus Christ is the perfect **sacrifice**. He is our **Savior**.

QUESTIONS: *Fill in the blanks.*

1. All people _____. They do not _____ God.
2. We cannot buy the _____ _____ _____.
3. Jesus Christ died for _____.
4. Jesus Christ is the perfect _____.

Give the answers.

5. Who is the plan of God for sin? _____
6. Why did Jesus die? To _____ us from sin.

Answer with a YES or NO. Circle the right answer.

7. Can people be friends with God if they sin?   YES or NO
8. Is the best **sacrifice** a blood **sacrifice?**   YES or NO
9. Do we still need to **sacrifice** animals today?   YES or NO
10. Did Jesus Christ die for you?   YES or NO

WORD LIST

1. **Bible times** *(noun phrase):* all the years that people in the Bible lived.
2. **cross** *(noun):* a tool used to kill people. A **cross** is made of wood in the shape of a T. People hung on a **cross** until they died.
3. **please** *(verb):* to make someone happy.
4. **sacrifice, sacrifices** *(noun):* a gift people give to God.
5. **save, saves** *(verb):* make free from sin.
6. **Savior** *(proper noun):* Jesus Christ; the One who saves us from sin and hell.

12   GOD FORGIVES OUR SINS

Important Bible Verse: "If we **confess** our sins, He [God] will **forgive** our sins. . . ." (1 John 1:9)

Jesus Christ was the one true sacrifice. His sacrifice was the plan of God to **forgive** our sins. Jesus gave His life for us. He is the Savior.

We can choose many things. The Bible says, ". . . You must choose for yourselves today whom you will serve. . . ." (Joshua 24:15) We can choose to become friends of God. We can choose to ask God to **forgive** us.

We must ask God for **forgiveness**. We must **confess** to God. We must tell Him that we are **sorry** for our sins. The Bible says, "The kind of sorrow God wants makes people change their hearts and lives. This leads to **salvation,** and you cannot be **sorry** for that. . . ." (2 Corinthians 7:10)

God **forgives** us when we **repent** of our sins. The Bible says, "If we **confess** our sins, He will **forgive** our sins. . . ." (1 John 1:9) He helps us not to sin. God helps us obey Him. He helps us to live by His laws.

We can also choose not to ask God for **forgiveness**. We can choose not to **repent**. But we will go to hell. We cannot live with God in heaven.

All sinners can **confess** and **repent**. Then, they receive the **forgiveness** of God. Then, sinners become Christians. They have the **salvation** of God. They are saved from sin and hell.

Another name for a Christian is **believer**. A **believer** believes in Jesus Christ. This person believes Jesus Christ is God. A **believer** obeys God. A **believer** is a friend of God.

God **forgives** our sins when we **confess** and **repent**. He makes our lives clean and new. The Bible says, "If anyone belongs to Christ, there is a new creation. The old things have gone; everything is made new!" (2 Corinthians 5:17) Then, we become children of God. We become a part of the family of God.

Are you **sorry** for your sins? You can **repent** right now. You can ask God to **forgive** your sins. You can become a **believer**. God wants to give you His **salvation**. Turn to page 36 and read lesson 16.

QUESTIONS: *Fill in the blanks.*

1. We can _____ to ask God to **forgive** our sins.
2. The Bible tells us that being **sorry** for our sins leads to
   _____. (See 2 Corinthians 7:10.)
3. God helps us not to _____.
4. Another name for a Christian is _____.
5. God _____ our sins when we **repent**.
   He makes our lives _____ and _____.
6. We become _____ of God. We become a
   part of the _____ of God.

Answer YES or NO. Circle the right answer for you.

7. Can I choose between right and wrong?   YES or NO
8. Have I **repented** of my sins?   YES or NO
9. Have I asked God to **forgive** my sins?   YES or NO
10. Will God help me obey Him?   YES or NO
11. Am I a child of God?   YES or NO
12. Is God my friend now?   YES or NO

WORD LIST

1. **believer** *(noun):* a Christian; a person who believes Jesus Christ is God; a person who **repents**.
2. **confess** *(verb):* tell God that we know we are sinners.
3. **forgive, forgives** *(verb):* choose to forget the wrong things that people do; make free from sin.
4. **forgiveness** *(noun):* God choosing to **forgive** our sins.
5. **repent, repented** *(verb):* stop doing sins; turned away from sin and turned to God.
6. **salvation** *(noun):* the act of God by which He saves people from sin.
7. **sorry** *(adjective):* be very sad about our sins.

13 JESUS CHRIST IS GOD

Important Bible Verse: "The Father and I are one." (John 10:30)

God knew that people were sinful. He knew that they needed His forgiveness. God knew a blood sacrifice was needed. Jesus Christ was that sacrifice.

The Bible tells us about the birth of Jesus. He had a human mother. The father of Jesus was God by the Holy Spirit. You can read this story in Luke 1:26-38 and 2:1-20.

The birth of Jesus Christ was a special birth. Christians remember His **birthday** every **Christmas. Christmas** is the **birthday** of Jesus.

Jesus Christ is God. And Jesus Christ is man. Only Jesus is God and man together. Jesus said, "The Father and I are one." (John 10:30)

Jesus Christ came for several **reasons.** He came to teach us. He came to show us the love of God. He came to die on a cross for our sins. The Bible says, "Christ Himself died for you. And that one death paid for your sins. . . . " (1 Peter 3:18)

Jesus Christ taught that we must obey God. Jesus said, ". . . If anyone loves Me, then he will obey My teaching. . . ." (John 14:23) Jesus Christ showed us how to please God. He obeyed God all the time. He pleased God, His Father.

Jesus Christ showed us the love of God. He loved people. He did miracles. He made sick people well. He did miracles to help people. Jesus said, ". . . I do miracles in My Father's name. Those miracles show who I am." (John 10:25)

QUESTIONS: *Fill in the blanks.*

1. God knew that people were sinful. They needed His

   _____.

2. Christians remember the **birthday** of Jesus every

   _____.

3. Jesus Christ said, "The Father and I are_____."

4. Jesus Christ taught that we must obey_____.

5. Jesus Christ said, "If anyone loves Me, then he will

   _____ _____ _____."

6. Jesus Christ did _____ to
   help people.

Give the answers.

7. Who was the father of Jesus Christ? _____

8. Who only is God and man together? _____

9. Why did Jesus Christ come to earth? Write three **reasons.**

   (1) _____

   (2) _____

   (3) _____

10. Who died on a cross for us? _____

WORD LIST

1. **birthday** *(noun):* the day a person is born.
2. **Christmas** *(proper noun):* a special day each year when we
   remember the **birthday** of Jesus Christ.
3. **miracles** *(noun):* things that happen only with the help of God.
4. **reasons** *(noun):* why people do what they do.

14 JESUS DIED, YET HE LIVES

Important Bible Verse: "God loved the world so much that He gave His one and only Son so that **whoever** believes in Him may not be **lost,** but have **eternal life.**" (John 3:16)

Jesus Christ died as a sacrifice. People needed a sacrifice because of their sins.

Jesus had no sin. He was the perfect sacrifice. He gave His life for us. He died on the Cross for our sins. The Bible says, "God shows His great love for us in this way: Christ died for us while we were still sinners." (Romans 5:8)

But Jesus Christ did not stay dead. God raised Him from death. God made Jesus live again. The Bible says, "We believe that Jesus died and that He rose again. . . ." (1 Thessalonians 4:14) This is called the **resurrection.** What a great miracle!

The death of Jesus shows that He is really human. The **resurrection** of Jesus shows that He is really God.

The **resurrection** of Jesus Christ shows His power. He frees sinners from sin. He saves them from their sins. This is the reason that Jesus died.

Jesus gives new life to all believers. He gives them **eternal life.** The Bible says, ". . . **whoever** believes in Him may not be lost, but have **eternal life.**" (John 3:16) **Whoever** means every person on earth. No person needs to be **lost.** All people can have **eternal life.**

Jesus Christ came back to life. He met with His believers many times. He told them, ". . . You will be My **witnesses** . . . in every part of the world." (Acts 1:8) Then, He returned to heaven. His believers watched Him go.

Jesus gave us two promises before He left. He promised to send the Holy Spirit. And He promised to return to earth one day.

Now Jesus is in heaven. He is with God the Father. Only Jesus can bring people and God together.

QUESTIONS: *Fill in the blanks.*

1. Jesus Christ had no _____. So He was the perfect _____.
2. Jesus Christ died on the _____ for our sins.
3. God raised Jesus Christ from _____. This is called the _____.
4. The death of Jesus shows He is really _____.
5. The **resurrection** of Jesus shows He is really _____.
6. Jesus Christ frees _____ from sin.

Give the answers.

7. What does Jesus give all believers? _____ _____
8. What did Jesus Christ say we are to be?

   _____
9. What did Jesus Christ promise before He left earth?
   (1) to send the _____ _____
   (2) to return to _____
10. Who is the only person who can bring people and God together? _____

WORD LIST

1. **eternal life** *(noun phrase):* the life that God gives; the life with God now and life with God forever in heaven.
2. **lost** *(adjective):* not able to find the way. **Lost** means someone who cannot find the way to heaven. A **lost** person is not a Christian.
3. **resurrection** *(noun):* return to life after death.
4. **whoever** *(pronoun):* all people; any person.
5. **witnesses** *(noun):* people who tell what Jesus Christ has done for them.

15 JESUS IS COMING AGAIN

Important Bible Verse: "... I will **come back** and take you to be with Me...." (John 14:3)

Jesus Christ told us to be His witnesses. We are witnesses when we tell people about Jesus Christ. We are witnesses when we work for Jesus. Then, other people may know about Him too. The Holy Spirit helps us to be witnesses.

We must be witnesses until Jesus returns to earth again. Jesus promised to **come back**. This is called the **Second Coming**. The **Second Coming** will be sudden.

The **Second Coming** is important for everyone. Jesus Christ will bring the judgment of God to all people. All people will be judged by God. Then, Christians will live with God in heaven forever. Sinners will live with Satan in hell forever.

Jesus Christ said, "... I will **come back** and take you to be with Me...." (John 14:3) No person knows when Jesus Christ will come. The Bible says, "... The **Son of Man** will come at a time you don't expect Him." (Matthew 24:44)

We must ask Jesus to be our Savior. We must live for Him each day. We must obey Him. Then, we will be ready for His return.

Are you ready for Jesus to **come back**?

Some people will die before the **Second Coming**. Believers will go to heaven. Sinners will go to hell. Are you ready to die? Are you ready for heaven? The Bible says, "So always be ready, because you don't know the day your Lord will come." (Matthew 24:42)

You can be ready for the **Second Coming**. You can be ready to die. Ask Jesus to save you. He wants to be your Savior and Friend.

QUESTIONS: *Fill in the blanks.*

1. Jesus Christ told us to be _____.
2. The _____ _____ helps us to be witnesses.
3. We must be witnesses until _____ returns to earth.
4. Jesus Christ promised to _____ _____.
5. The _____ _____ is when Jesus **comes back** to earth.
6. After the **Second Coming,** all people will be _____ by God.

Answer YES or NO. Circle the right answer.

7. Is Jesus Christ coming to earth again?   YES or NO
8. Will sinners live with God in heaven?   YES or NO
9. Do we know when Jesus will **come back?**   YES or NO
10. Will all people be alive when Jesus returns?   YES or NO
11. Can we be ready for Jesus to **come back?**   YES or NO
12. Are you ready for the **Second Coming?**   YES or NO

WORD LIST

1. **come back, comes back** *(verb phrase):* return; come again.
2. **Second Coming** *(proper noun phrase):* when Jesus Christ **comes back** to earth again.
3. **Son of Man** *(proper noun phrase):* Jesus Christ, who was born of a human mother. Jesus is both the Son of God and the **Son of Man.**

16 HOW TO BECOME A CHRISTIAN

Are you a Christian? Will you go to heaven when you die? Do you know that Jesus saves you now?

Is your answer "yes"? That is great! But is your answer "no"? Then, you can become a Christian. You can be saved right now.

Here is what you must do:

1. You must believe that Jesus Christ is the Savior. You must believe that He can save you.

    "... Believe in the Lord Jesus and you will be saved ..." (Acts 16:31)

2. You must tell Jesus that you are sorry for your sins.

    "The kind of sorrow God wants makes people change their hearts and lives. This leads to salvation ..." (2 Corinthians 7:10)

3. You must repent. You must change the way that you are living.

    "You must change your hearts and lives! Come back to God, and He will forgive your sins." (Acts 3:19)

4. You must ask Jesus to forgive your sins.

    "Forgive us for our sins ..." (Luke 11:4)

5. You must believe that God forgives you through Jesus Christ.

    "All who believe in Jesus' name will be forgiven of their sins through Jesus' name." (Acts 10:43)

6. You must **accept** Jesus. You must receive Him into your heart and life.

    "To all who did **accept** Him and believe in Him He gave the **right** to become children of God." (John 1:12)

Would you pray this prayer?

God, I know I am a sinner. I have sinned against You. I am sorry for my sins. I repent of my sins. Forgive me for all my sins. I now believe that You forgive me.

Come into my life. Help me not to sin again. I **accept** Jesus Christ as my Savior. I receive Him into my heart and life. Thank You, God. I now have the **right** to be Your child. **Amen.**

Now, tell another person today that Jesus Christ saves you. The Bible says, "I [Jesus] tell you, all those who stand before others and say they believe in Me, I, the Son of Man, will say before the angels of God that they belong to Me. . . ." (Luke 12:8) You should tell other people about your salvation. You should tell what Jesus has done for you. This will help you grow as a Christian.

WORD LIST

1. **accept** *(verb):* agree to receive; agree in your mind and heart.
2. **amen** *(interjection):* a word used at the end of prayers. **Amen** means *yes, it is true.* **Amen** shows that we agree with what was said.
3. **right** *(noun):* something that we can say is ours. We have the **right** not to be hurt by another person. As Christians, we have the **right** to be children of God.

TEACHING RESOURCES

The *intercultural English lessons* in this book are written for people who are developing proficiency in English. The intended audience includes bilingual speakers, such as new immigrants and ESL (English as a second language) learners, and English speakers who are new readers or learning disabled. Also, new Christians and people with a limited knowledge of Bible truths can benefit by the simple, brief lessons. Such people can profit from materials with a controlled vocabulary and sentence structure to help them better understand the Bible and Christian concepts. These lessons are designed to serve as transition materials while the learners are gaining Bible knowledge and English skills.

The target audience is the beginning-level student who can work comfortably with a 450-word vocabulary. The writers, therefore, gave careful consideration to both the vocabulary and sentence structure.

New words and phrases, less than 10, are introduced in each lesson. The words/phrases are in the word lists in the same form or forms as in the lesson text. The parts of speech are included as an aid for teaching English.

In applying linguistic controls, the language is simplified. The writers purposely sacrificed style for simplicity to obtain English at a level that is more easily read by the target audience.

There are three appendixes in this section, *Teaching Resources.* Appendix A contains suggested answers to the study questions and additional scriptures. Appendix B includes all the vocabulary introduced in the lessons. Appendix C has several useful tips for teaching. Teachers should become familiar with this supplementary information.

Teachers need to be sensitive to the work of the Holy Spirit. Lesson 16, "How to Become a Christian," may be used at any time a student is ready to accept Jesus Christ as Savior.

I believe this simple Bible study material meets a vital need in Christian churches today. I pray that God will honor His Word as it becomes a part of the learners' minds and hearts.

—Editor

APPENDIX A

ANSWERS TO QUESTIONS AND ADDITIONAL SCRIPTURES

The information in this appendix is provided to help the teacher in teaching the lessons in this book.

For each lesson, there is a set of suggested answers for the study questions. You will find the intended answers, along with some possible alternatives (in parentheses), which are all correct in the context of the lessons. Teachers should accept any answer that can be justified.

There is also a list of additional scriptures for each lesson. These will provide biblical support for the Christian beliefs and doctrines that are presented. Teachers may use these for background reading in teaching the lessons. Students who are literate in a language other than English will benefit from reading these scriptures in their own Bibles.

Please read the "Note" in Lesson 12 in this appendix. Although the statement is appropriate for that particular lesson, it can apply to any of the lessons. Teachers should be sensitive to the Holy Spirit as He works in the hearts of the students.

LESSON 1

Answers to Questions:
1. God
2. any other gods
3. God
4. choose
5. Father; Lord; King
6. God
7. God
8. God
9. earth; people
10. true (powerful; good; great; only)

Additional Scriptures:
Exodus 20:2-4
Numbers 23:19
Deuteronomy 5:6-8
Deuteronomy 6:4
Deuteronomy 32:6
1 Chronicles 16:25-29
Psalm 95:3
Psalm 100
Psalm 121
Psalm 145:8-9
Isaiah 44:6-8
Jeremiah 10:10
Jeremiah 32:18-19
Acts 17:24-29
1 Corinthians 8:5-6
1 Timothy 6:15
James 2:19

LESSON 2

Answers to Questions:
1. world
2. Creator
3. everything (all things)
4. life
5. important
6. creation
7. God
8. Bible
9. day (night; sky; earth; land; water; plants; animals; people)
10. soil; earth

Additional Scriptures:
Genesis 1 and 2
Genesis 5:1-2
Deuteronomy 32:6
Psalm 33:6-9
Psalm 95:3-7
Psalm 104:24
Psalm 121:2
Isaiah 40:28
Jeremiah 32:17
Mark 13:19
Acts 17:24
Colossians 1:15-17
1 Timothy 4:4
Hebrews 1:10
Revelation 10:6

LESSON 3

Answers to Questions:
1. lived (been alive)
2. beginning; end
3. everywhere
4. powerful
5. world
6. eternal
7. everywhere
8. God
9. God
10. eternal; everywhere; powerful; all things

Additional Scriptures:
Genesis 21:33
Job 42:1-2
Psalm 139:1-4
Psalm 139:7-10
Proverbs 15:3
Isaiah 40:28
Isaiah 44:6
Isaiah 48:12
Jeremiah 10:10
Jeremiah 23:24
Jeremiah 32:17
Matthew 12:25
Matthew 19:26
John 2:24
Ephesians 3:20-21
1 John 3:20
1 John 4:4
Revelation 1:8

LESSON 4

Answers to Questions:
1. holy (perfect; loving)
2. evil
3. love
4. very much
5. peace
6. God
7. holy
8. true God
9. content
10. peace

Additional Scriptures:
Leviticus 11:44-45
Leviticus 20:7
Deuteronomy 7:9
Psalm 29:11
Psalm 62:11-12
Psalm 145:8-9
Isaiah 5:16
Isaiah 6:3
Isaiah 9:6
Isaiah 43:15
Luke 1:49
John 3:16
John 16:33
Philippians 4:7
2 Thessalonians 3:16
1 Peter 1:15
1 John 4:10-12

Matthew 16:13-16
John 1:1-2
John 4:24
John 10:34-38
John 14:6-11
John 14:26
John 16:7-15
John 17:1-5
1 Corinthians 8:6
2 Corinthians 13:14
Galatians 1:1-5
Galatians 4:4-6
Philippians 2:5-11
1 Thessalonians 4:8
Hebrews 1:1-5
Hebrews 4:14
1 John 1:3
1 John 4:2-3
1 John 4:11-16

LESSON 5

Answers to Questions:
1. God
2. He loves us
3. Jesus (Christ)
4. know
5. Father; Son; Holy Spirit
6. God
7. triune
8. God (the Father)
9. Jesus (Christ)
10. Holy Spirit

Additional Scriptures:
Deuteronomy 32:6
Isaiah 11:2
Isaiah 48:16
Isaiah 61:1
Matthew 3:16-17
Matthew 11:27

Lesson 6

Answers to Questions:
1. Holy Bible
2. Scripture
3. Old Testament
4. New Testament
5. inspired
6. everything we need
7. 66
8. (Holy) Bible
9. all Scripture
10. (Holy) Bible

Additional Scriptures:
Exodus 20:1-17
Exodus 24:3-4
Exodus 34:27-28
Psalm 1:2
Psalm 19:7-11

Psalm 33:4-5
Isaiah 40:8
Jeremiah 30:2
Matthew 5:17-18
Mark 13:31
Luke 11:28
Luke 24:44-49
Romans 1:1-4
1 Corinthians 15:3-5
2 Timothy 2:15
2 Timothy 3:14-17
Hebrews 4:12
2 Peter 1:20-21

LESSON 7

Answers to Questions:
1. teaches (tells)
2. live
3. loves
4. cares
5. protect
6. read; study
7. God
8. (Holy) Bible
9. we (anyone can)
10. (Holy) Bible

Additional Scriptures:
Deuteronomy 6:4-9
Joshua 1:8-9
Psalm 19:7-11
Psalm 37:28, 40
Psalm 119:9-11
Psalm 119:105-106
Psalm 119:129-130
Nahum 1:7
Luke 11:28
Luke 24:44-47
John 3:16

Ephesians 6:13-17
2 Timothy 2:15
2 Timothy 3:14-17
Hebrews 4:12

LESSON 8

Answers to Questions:
1. sin
2. obey
3. nature
4. sinful
5. separates
6. Adam; Eve
7. friend of God
8. tempted
9. we are (all people)
10. (our) sins

Additional Scriptures:
Genesis 1:26-27
Genesis 3:1-20
Genesis 6:5
Psalm 51:1-5
Proverbs 5:22
Jeremiah 17:9
Matthew 4:1-11
Mark 7:20-23
Romans 1:18-25
Romans 5:12-13
Romans 7:14-25
1 Corinthians 10:13
Galatians 5:16-21
Ephesians 2:1-3
James 1:13-15
1 John 1:8

LESSON 9

Answers to Questions:
1. born

2. Adam; Eve
3. good lives
4. disobeying (breaking; not obeying; choosing not to obey)
5. sin
6. all (people; Adam and Eve)
7. Ten Commandments
8. sinners
9. Yes
10. Yes
11. No
12. No

Additional Scriptures:
Exodus 34:27-28
Deuteronomy 5:6-21
1 Kings 8:46
Proverbs 20:9
Ecclesiastes 7:20
Matthew 15:18-20
Matthew 22:36-40
John 8:34
Romans 1:28-31
Romans 3:9-12
Romans 7:14-25
Galatians 5:16-21
Ephesians 2:1-3
1 John 1:8-10
1 John 3:8

LESSON 10
Answers to Questions:
1. sin
2. death
3. judge
4. heaven; hell
5. heaven

6. good works
7. holy
8. plan
9. No
10. Yes
11. No
12. No

Additional Scriptures:
1 Samuel 2:10
Psalm 7:8-9
Psalm 9:8
Psalm 50:6
Psalm 96:10, 13
Psalm 98:9
Isaiah 33:22
Matthew 25:31-46
Mark 9:42-48
Luke 16:19-26
John 5:25-30
John 14:2-3
Acts 17:30-31
Romans 2:12-13, 16
Romans 3:23-25
Romans 6:23
1 Corinthians 15:35-55
2 Corinthians 5:10
2 Thessalonians 1:5-10
2 Timothy 4:1, 8
Hebrews 10:30
Revelation 20:11-15

LESSON 11
Answers to Questions:
1. sin; obey
2. love of God
3. everyone (all people)
4. sacrifice
5. Jesus (Christ)

6. save
7. No
8. Yes
9. No
10. Yes

Additional Scriptures:
Exodus 29:10-14
Leviticus, chapters 4—5
Leviticus 6:24-30
Leviticus 14:19-22, 30-31
Psalm 50:14
Psalm 54:6
Isaiah 53:5-6
Matthew 27:11-66
Mark 10:45
John 1:29
John 3:16-17
John 19:16-37
Acts 4:10-12
Romans 3:23-26
1 Corinthians 6:20
Galatians 3:13-14
Ephesians 2:13
Colossians 1:19-20
1 Timothy 2:3-6
Hebrews 7:22-28
Hebrews 9:11-15
Hebrews 9:26-28
Hebrews 10:1-14
Hebrews 13:12
1 Peter 1:18-21
1 John 2:1-2

LESSON 12

Answers to Questions:
1. choose
2. salvation
3. sin
4. believer
5. forgives; clean; new
6. children (friends); family
7. Yes
8. [personal response]
9. [personal response]
10. Yes
11. [personal response]
12. [personal response]

Additional Scriptures:
2 Chronicles 7:14
Psalm 32:5
Psalm 51:1-17
Isaiah 55:6-7
Ezekiel 18:30-32
Ezekiel 33:14-16
Mark 1:14-15
Luke 13:1-5
Acts 2:38-39
Acts 3:19-20
Acts 13:38-39
Acts 17:30
Romans 3:21-26
Romans 4:7-8
Romans 5:1-2
Romans 8:1-4
Romans 8:12-17
Galatians 3:26-29
Galatians 4:4-7
Colossians 2:13-14
Titus 3:4-7
2 Peter 3:9
1 John 3:1-2
1 John 5:1

NOTE: If a student shows a readiness to become a Christian, you may turn to Lesson 16 and help him/her

44

with the six steps and prayer printed there. Then you may continue in the next class session with the lesson material you have not presented.

LESSON 13

Answers to Questions:
1. forgiveness
2. Christmas
3. one
4. God
5. obey my teaching
6. miracles
7. God
8. Jesus (Christ)
9. (1) to teach us; (2) to show us the love of God; (3) to die for us on a cross
10. Jesus (Christ)

Additional Scriptures:
Matthew 1:18-25
Matthew 16:15-16
Luke 1:26-38
Luke 2:1-20
John 1:1-5
John 1:10-14
John 6:35-40
Acts 5:29-31
Romans 1:2-6
Romans 5:6-8
Romans 8:3-4
Galatians 4:4-5
Philippians 2:5-11
Titus 2:11-14
Hebrews 1:1-5
1 John 1:3

1 John 4:14-19

LESSON 14

Answers to Questions:
1. sin; sacrifice
2. Cross
3. death; resurrection
4. human
5. God
6. sinners (people)
7. new life (eternal life)
8. (My) witnesses
9. (1) Holy Spirit (2) earth
10. Jesus (Christ)

Additional Scriptures:
Matthew 28:1-10
Matthew 28:16-20
Mark 16:6
Mark 16:9-16, 19
Luke 24:1-7
Luke 24:36-49
John 11:25-26
John 14:3
John 14:15-17
John 14:26-28
John 15:26-27
John 16:7-11
Acts 1:6-11
Acts 4:33
Acts 5:30
Romans 1:2-4
1 Peter 1:3-5
1 Peter 3:18-22

LESSON 15

Answers to Questions:
1. witnesses
2. Holy Spirit

3. Jesus (Christ)
4. come back (come again; return)
5. Second Coming
6. judged
7. Yes
8. No
9. No
10. No
11. Yes
12. [personal response]

Additional Scriptures:
Matthew 16:27-28
Matthew 24:27, 30-31
Matthew 24:36-42
Matthew 25:13
Matthew 25:31-46
Matthew 28:19-20
Mark 16:15-16
Luke 12:8-9
Luke 21:25-28
John 14:1-3
Acts 1:8-11
Philippians 3:20-21
1 Thessalonians 4:15-18
1 Thessalonians 5:1-3
Titus 2:11-14
Hebrews 9:27-28
2 Peter 3:10-13
Revelation 12:11
Revelation 22:7, 20

LESSON 16

Answers to Questions: [None]

Additional Scriptures: [None]

APPENDIX B
WORD LIST

Below is an alphabetical list of all the words and phrases in the Word Lists in this book. The numbers [in brackets] following each entry indicate the lessons where the words were introduced.

accept *(verb):* agree to receive; agree in your mind and heart. [16]

Alpha *(noun):* the first letter in the Greek alphabet. **Alpha** means the beginning. [3]

amen *(interjection):* a word used at the end of prayers. **Amen** means *yes, it is true.* **Amen** shows that we agree with what was said. [16]

believer *(noun):* a **Christian**; a person who believes Jesus Christ is God; a person who **repents**. [12]

Bible *(proper noun):* the book God gave us to learn about Him. [1]

Bible times *(noun phrase):* all the years that people in the **Bible** lived. [11]

birthday *(noun):* the day a person is born. [13]

break the law, breaks the law, breaking the law *(verb phrase):* **disobey** God; do not obey the laws of God. [9]

builder *(noun):* a person who builds or makes something. [2]

caused *(verb):* made to happen. [2]

Christian, Christians *(proper noun):* a person who believes Jesus Christ is the Son of God; people who follow and obey Jesus Christ. [6]

Christmas *(proper noun):* a special day each year when we remember the **birthday** of Jesus Christ. [13]

come back, comes back *(verb phrase):* return; come again. [15]

confess *(verb):* tell God that we know we are **sinners**. [12]

content *(adjective):* happy; full of joy. [4]

created *(verb):* made something from nothing. [2]

creation *(noun):* everything God has made. [2]

Creator *(proper noun):* a name for God, who made all things. [2]

cross *(noun):* a tool used to kill people. A **cross** is made of wood in the shape of a T. People hung on a **cross** until they died. [11]

difficult *(adjective):* not easy; hard to do. [7]

disobey, disobeying *(verb):* do not obey; not obeying. [9]

encourage, encourages *(verb):* make someone feel better; helps and guides. [5]

eternal *(adjective):* has no beginning or end; has always lived and will always live. [3]

eternal life *(noun phrase):* the life that God gives; the life with God now and life with God forever in **heaven**. [14]

everywhere *(adverb):* all places. [3]

evil *(adjective):* very bad; not good. [4]

forgive, forgives *(verb):* choose to forget the wrong things that people do; make free from **sin**. [12]

forgiveness *(noun):* God choosing to **forgive** our **sins**. [12]

gods *(noun):* false **gods**; not the one true God. [1]

good works *(noun phrase):* what we do to help other people; kind deeds. [10]

greater *(adjective):* more great; with more power. [2]

heaven *(noun):* the place where God is; the home of God. [10]

hell *(noun):* a place where people are punished forever for their **sins**; the home of **sinners** after death. [10]

hidden *(adjective):* not seen with the eyes; not in sight. [3]

Himself *(pronoun):* God talking as God. [6]

inspired *(verb):* gave thoughts to; guided the mind. [6]

judgment *(noun):* when God will judge all people; when God says who goes to **heaven** or **hell**. [10]

Lord *(proper noun):* another name for God. [1]

lost *(adjective):* not able to find the way. **Lost** means someone who cannot find the way to **heaven**. A **lost** person is not a **Christian**. [14]

loving *(adjective):* full of love. [4]

miracles *(noun):* things that happen only with the help of God. [13]

nature *(noun):* the real self; what a person is inside his being. [8]

Omega *(noun):* the last letter in the Greek alphabet. **Omega** means the end. [3]

ourselves *(pronoun):* us; you and me. [10]

perfect *(adjective):* without **evil**; does nothing wrong; does not make mistakes. [4]

please *(verb):* to make someone happy. [11]

powerful *(adjective):* full of power; very strong. [1]

protect *(verb):* care for; keep safe. [7]

reasons *(noun):* why people do what they do. [13]

repent, repented *(verb):* stop doing **sins**; turned away from **sin** and turned to God. [12]

resurrection *(noun):* return to life after death. [14]

right *(noun):* something that we can say is ours. We have the **right** not to be hurt by another person. As **Christians,** we have the **right** to be children of God. [16]

sacred *(adjective):* holy; belonging to God. [6]

sacrifice, sacrifices *(noun):* a gift people give to God. [11]

salvation *(noun):* the act of God by which He **saves** people from **sin.** [12]

Satan *(proper noun):* the most **powerful** of **evil** spirits; **Satan** is against God and people. [8]

save, saves *(verb):* make free from **sin.** [11]

Savior *(proper noun):* Jesus Christ; the One who **saves** us from **sin** and **hell.** [11]

Scripture *(proper noun):* **sacred written** words; special **written** words from God to all people; the Holy **Bible** for **Christians.** [6]

Second Coming *(proper noun phrase):* when Jesus Christ **comes back** to earth again. [15]

separates, separated *(verb):* not together; apart; in two different places. [8]

sin, sins *(noun):* **evil;** wrong acts. **sin, sinned** *(verb):* do wrong acts; did not obey God. [8]

sinful *(adjective):* full of **sin.** [8]

sinful nature *(noun phrase):* the part of people that makes them **sin.** [8]

sinners *(noun):* people who **sin;** people who do not obey the laws of God. [9]

Son of Man *(proper noun phrase):* Jesus Christ, who was born of a human mother. Jesus is both the Son of God and the **Son of Man.** [15]

sorry *(adjective):* be very sad about our **sins.** [12]

tempts, tempted *(verb):* tests; tried to get people to **sin** or do wrong. [8]

terrible *(adjective):* very, very bad. [10]

three in one *(noun phrase):* three parts of one thing; the **triune** God. [5]

triune *(adjective):* **three in one**; God is God in three persons: God the Father, God the Son, and God the Holy Spirit. [5]

useful *(adjective):* can be used; of help; helpful. [7]

whoever *(pronoun):* all people; any person. [14]

witnesses *(noun):* people who tell what Jesus Christ has done for them. [14]

worship *(verb):* to honor God; to praise and serve God. [1]

written *(adjective):* in writing; put on paper so people can read. [6]

APPENDIX C
TEACHING HELPS

A. **Plan carefully and prayerfully.** Anything important enough to do is important enough to plan to do. Unplanned teaching usually results in disorganized instruction, resulting in minimal learning. A familiar maxim says, "If I fail to plan, I plan to fail." Your students are worthy of your careful planning and sincere prayers. Commit your teaching and the learners to God. He will help you as you do your best.

B. **Be sensitive to the learners' needs.** Your students will probably be at different levels, both in their Bible knowledge and language skills. Your task, which is not an easy one, is to discover where the learners are in their English skills and in their understanding of the Christian faith.

Be aware, also, that the learners' *felt needs* may be different from their *real needs.* But their *felt needs* usually must be met first before you are able to help them with their *real needs.* In your class, you may find that the *felt need* is to learn to read, while the *real need* is to learn about God. And while you strive to meet the perceived or *felt need,* never lose sight of the *real need.*

There is no special method to help you make this discovery. You DO need to become a people-watcher, however. Look for any hints the students may give in their body language and in what they say. Also, become involved in the learners' lives, both in and out of class. This will help you become much more aware of their backgrounds, their culture, their experiences, and, thus, their needs, *felt and real.* God will be faithful as you commit this *discovery process* to Him.

C. **Determine your objective.** An objective is the purpose for teaching. Your objective or aim, as a Christian teacher, is twofold: Bible content and English language skills. Knowing *what* you are teaching, and *why,* will help you be more confident as a teacher or tutor. As a result, your instruction will be more effective. Therefore, become familiar with the lesson content and, if possible, the language skills needed by the learners.

D. **Focus on comprehension.** This is extremely important! If the learners do not understand, your instruction will be of limited value. Of course, every student will not fully understand everything you teach. But, as a teacher or tutor, try to have each student take away some learning from each session. How much the students understand and learn will vary from person to person. Yet, as a teacher or tutor, your task is to faithfully plant the seeds of God's Word. Then the Holy Spirit will help those seeds to grow and bear fruit in the minds and hearts of the learners.

Some strategies for aiding comprehension are:

1. *Use easy-to-understand Bibles.* Some recommended ones are:

   - *The Holy Bible, New Century Version.* Thomas Nelson, Inc., P.O. Box 141000, Nashville, TN 37214

   - *Contemporary English Version.* American Bible Society, 101 North Independence Mall East FL8, Philadelphia, PA 19106-2155

   - *The Good News Translation Bible.* American Bible Society, 101 North Independence Mall East FL8, Philadelphia, PA 19106-2155

   - *Holy Bible: New Life Version.* Barbour Publishing, 1810 Barbour Dr. SE, Uhrichsville, OH 44683

   If the students are not native speakers of English, have the students read the Scripture in their first language. This will certainly aid their understanding. Some sources of Bibles in various languages are:

   - American Bible Society, 101 North Independence Mall East FL8 Philadelphia, PA 19106-2155

   - Multi-Language Media, 701 Pennsylvania Ave, Fort Washington, PA 19034

   - International Bible Society, 1820 Jet Stream Drive, Colorado Springs, CO 80921

- Bible League International, 1 Bible League Plaza, Crete, IL 60417

2. *Use the students' first language also, if their native language is other than English.* This is ideal and will result in the greatest amount of learning. If an interpreter is available, or if you know the language, use both languages in your teaching. If possible, give the interpreter the material to be taught before the class session so he or she can become familiar with the lesson content.

3. *Take additional time to teach a lesson, as needed.* You can divide a lesson into two or more parts, according to the needs of the learners. *Remember:* You're teaching people, not materials. Materials are only tools by which you accomplish your objectives or aims.

4. *Tell the learners what you plan to teach as you begin a lesson.* Make the students aware of the lesson content at the beginning of the class. Then after you have taught, give a brief review. Thus, the lesson plan should include these three steps: (1) telling what you are going to teach, (2) teaching, and (3) telling what you have just taught.

5. *Involve the students as much as possible.* Most people learn best by doing. Therefore, involve the students in a wide variety of activities: listening, talking, moving, drawing, devising, singing, discussing, cooperating, writing, conversing, exploring, memorizing, manipulating, creating, reciting, etc. Take advantage of all the possible ways students learn.

6. *Use the questions in the lessons as a part of your teaching.* Questions are an important part of teaching. If time permits, use the questions as a part of the lessons. Or if time is limited, assign the questions for home study and discuss them during the next class session as review and reinforcement. Avoid grading the answers in such a way that the students have a sense of failure. (See Section E.) *Note:* If the questions are an out-of-class assignment, be aware that other family members or friends may help answer the questions.

7. *Don't assume the learners can read the lessons on their own.* If the learners cannot read English, teach the lessons orally. Once the students seem to be reading independently, don't assume they understand what they are reading. Pronouncing the words does not necessarily mean they can read with comprehension. Use oral questions and discussion to help you determine how much they understand.

8. *Work with new and unknown words both before and during the lesson.* Develop vocabulary in meaningful activities, avoiding word lists. Many of the high-frequency words of English (such as *the, but, or, of, by, because*) have limited or no meaning by themselves. Also, many nouns and verbs have multiple meanings. Vocabulary has little value if there are no useful meanings for the learners. Always work with words in phrases or sentences that have meaning for the students. Make flash cards by writing the new word on the front, and write sentences with the word on the back. Also, be careful in the use of idioms, figures of speech, and slang expressions.

9. *Add your own examples and stories that are appropriate for the lessons.* Nonbiblical examples and stories are not included, since such examples and stories are different from culture to culture. Yet, such stories or examples are very effective in the learning process. Just make certain the stories, examples, or illustrations are appropriate and meaningful for your learners.

10. *Use real objects, pictures, and other audiovisual aids, as much as possible.* Bulletin boards, charts, flash cards, models, photographs, videos, etc., will make the lessons more effective.

E. **Teach for success.** This begins, of course, with focusing on comprehension. If the learners understand, then you should expect success.

1. *Give sincere praise.* Help the students know they are learning. Reinforce their self-worth as individuals and as God's children, created in His image.

2. *Capitalize on the learners' strengths and their correct responses.* Minimize their weaknesses and mistakes.

3. *Assume every student WANTS to learn, CAN learn, and WILL learn.* Then teach according to this belief.

F. **Be a good language model.** This is essential, since people are introduced to language by listening to it. This is true for all native and most nonnative English speakers. As a language model, however, you do not have to be perfect. Discard any worries you may have. Just be yourself and be the best you can be. Try these practical ideas:

1. *Be natural.* Use spoken English as it is naturally used by native English speakers. Be careful not to talk down to the learners by using "baby talk."

2. *Talk slowly.* Most learners, especially second-language learners, better understand language if spoken a little slower than used in normal speech. Yet, the speaker must maintain appropriate volume, rhythm, stress, and phrasing. Some teachers err by increasing volume as they slow down their speech. The increased volume is often misinterpreted by the learners.

3. *Be clear in pronunciation.* Pronounce words distinctly, making certain that you do not omit or slur final consonant sounds. Try to be clear and precise in your pronunciation while retaining naturalness.

   Don't expect adults or older youth who are learning English as a second language to speak it as native speakers. Research indicates that the learners will probably always speak it with an accent. *Remember:* The goal is for the learners to be able to communicate in English. They can accomplish this goal even if their pronunciation is not perfect.

4. *Model correct language.* This is an important technique, especially for correcting mistakes. You can show the correct response, language usage, or pronunciation simply by "doing it" yourself. Don't require the students to correct all their mistakes. For each lesson, focus on

only one or two mistakes you would like the learners to correct and master. Pointing out too many errors at a time can be discouraging and embarrassing for learners.

5. *Read aloud often.* You, as the teacher or tutor, can model good reading and oral language as you read aloud to the students. Research indicates that this is a valuable technique. As you read, be expressive and enthusiastic.

   Students need to hear you read the Scriptures frequently as well as the entire lesson. Read a Bible passage or the lesson aloud first before the learners ever see it. Then, read it a second time while they follow along with their eyes. This provides them with needed auditory (ear) and visual (eye) introduction to the lesson before they read it on their own.

Editor's Note:

This information on teaching is extremely limited. Entire textbooks have been written on this subject. Space requirements, however, require that this supplementary material be brief. I pray, though, that what you have read will assist you as you minister to your students.

J. Wesley Eby

NOTES

NOTES

NOTES

NOTES

NOTES

NOTES

NOTES

NOTES

www.ingramcontent.com/pod-product-compliance
Lightning Source LLC
Chambersburg PA
CBHW071932020426

42331CB00010B/2832